STANDARD COMPANION
to

CARNIVAL GLASS

IDENTIFICATION & VALUES

THIRD EDITION

MIKE CARWILE

COLLECTOR BOOKS

A Division of Schroeder Publishing Co., Inc.

Front Cover: Grape Leaves bowl, Northwood, 1909 – 1910, $95.00

Cover design by Beth Summers
Book design by Marty Turner

COLLECTOR BOOKS

P. O. Box 3009
Paducah, Kentucky 42002-3009

www.collectorbooks.com

Copyright © 2007 Mike Carwile

The current values in this book should be used only as a guide. They are not intended to set prices, which vary from one section of the country to another. Auction prices as well as dealer prices vary greatly and are affected by condition as well as demand. Neither the author nor the publisher assumes responsibility for any losses that might be incurred as a result of consulting this guide.

Searching for a Publisher?

We are always looking for people knowledgeable within their fields. If you feel that there is a real need for a book on your collectible subject and have a large comprehensive collection, contact Collector Books.

Proudly printed and bound in the
United States of America

Dedication

I would like to take this opportunity to dedicate this, my first solo edition, to someone who has not only been an inspiration to me, but a person that I can truly say is my best friend in all of carnival glass. To Bill Edwards, thank you from the bottom of my heart. I hope you will enjoy many years of retirement and relaxation; you deserve it.

Preface

This third edition of the *Standard Companion to Carnival Glass* has all new patterns and doesn't repeat any from the first or second editions; thus, it becomes a companion in fact as well as name.

While the first edition dealt with primary patterns and the second edition went into patterns that are a bit harder to find, as well as advertising pieces, I've decided to show a mix of patterns in this third edition, including a few non-American patterns that did not make it into the previously released *Standard Companion to Non-American Carnival Glass*.

Once again I am using the abbreviated format with only vital information of pattern name, maker, date of production, reproductions (if any have been reported to date), shapes, colors, and values.

I certainly thank all the collectors who purchased the first and second editions, especially newer collectors, many who have written to say they found these useful books, and I hope they will be just as happy with this edition.

Again, let me say this is just a guide and doesn't establish prices which fluctuate from one area to another. Remember, carnival glass has to be graded by the buyer as to condition, rarity, desirability, and quality of iridescence. No price guide can tell you what you should invest in a piece of glass.

Contents

Contents

The Basics of Carnival Glass Collecting

First comes color. To tell the true color of a piece of carnival glass, hold the piece to a strong light; the base color you see is the color of the piece. The colors given off by the iridescence have little or nothing to do with the true color of the glass. Many have asked me to provide a color chart to aid beginners, but capturing glass colors on paper is nearly impossible. The best advice I can offer on color is to handle as much of this glass as you can, holding it to the light and observing; soon, colors will come naturally, at least the basic colors.

Next, perhaps I should discuss shapes. Bowls and plates are easy to understand as are pitchers, tumblers, and vases; but even those have variations: bowls can be ruffled, unruffled (shallow unruffled bowls are called ice cream shape), deep, or shallow. Pitchers can be standard, smaller (milk pitcher), taller (tankard), or squat. Tumblers can be standard size, tall (lemonade), or small (juice), even as small as shot glasses. Vases can range from tiny 4" bud vases to monster 22" sizes called funeral vases. Vases may be straight topped, flared, or JIP (jack-in-the-pulpit) shaped with one side down and one side up. In addition there are table sets, consisting of a creamer, a sugar, a covered butter dish, and a spooner (this piece has no lid). There are decanters and stemmed goblets of several sizes; there are rose bowls, evident by the lips being pulled in equally around the top of the piece; candy dishes that have the rims flared out; and nut bowls that have the rim standing straight up. There are banana bowls that are pulled up on two sides, baskets that have handles, bonbons that have handles on opposite sides, and nappies with only one handle. In addition we have berry sets (small and large bowls that are deep and usually come with one large bowl and six small ones), orange bowls (large footed bowls that held fruit), handled mugs, and plates (these are shallow without any bowl effect, coming straight out from the base and no higher from base to rim than 2"). Specialized shapes include candlesticks, hatpins, hatpin holders (footed pieces with the rim turned in to hold hatpins), epergnes (pieces that hold flower lilies), card trays (flattened bonbons or nappies), toothpick holders, cracker and cookie jars with lids, stemmed compotes (or comports as they were originally called), hair receivers, powder jars with lids, as well as many, many novelties that include paperweights, animal novelties, and wall pocket vases. Finally we have punch sets which consist of a punch bowl, standard or base, and matching cups. These are all the general shapes of carnival glass. In addition we have many specialty shapes that include light shades, beads, beaded purses, odd whimsey shapes of all sorts that have been fashioned from standard pieces, pintrays, dresser trays, pickle casters in metal frames, and bride's baskets likewise. The list of shapes is almost endless and the beginner should study these and ask other collectors about odd pieces that can't be identified.

Now, let's talk briefly about the iridescence itself. By far the major portion of carnival glass items will be found with a satiny finish that has many colored highlights across the surface, like oil on water; but another very popular finish was developed by the Millersburg Company and used by all other makers in limited amounts. This is called "radium" finish and can be recognized by its shiny, mirror-like lustre on the surface. Often, with radium finish, the exterior of the piece has no iridization and the piece has a light, watery shine. Beyond that, some colors, especially pastels such as white, ice blue, and ice green, have a frosty look. This treatment is always satin, never radium. Finally, there is the addition of the milky edge on treatments that are called opalescent. Added to the marigold finish, this is called "peach opalescent" and with the ice blue, it becomes "aqua opalescent." Other opalescent treatments with carnival glass are blue opalescent, amethyst opalescent, lime green opalescent, ice green opalescent, vaseline opalescent, and red opalescent.

Finally, there are many new color labels that have come about over the last few years. These are mostly shadings of primary or secondary colors; they are often hard to understand and harder to describe. Here are a few: moonstone (opaque glass, not as dense as milk glass); clambroth (pale ginger ale color); black amethyst (nearly black glass iridized); horehound (a shade darker than amber); Persian blue (opaque, like moonstone but blue); smoke (grayish, with blue and gold highlights); teal (a mixture of blue and green); vaseline (a mixture of green and yellow); lavender (a pale amethyst); and lime (green with a yellow mix). Lastly, there are a handful of colors, now in vogue, that nobody seems to agree on a definition: things like Renniger blue, a tealish, sapphirey blue, according to some! Have I carried all this too far? Of course, but it isn't in my hands to stop this proliferation of colors. I can only hope the above information proves helpful in some way. Remember, we are all learning and knowledge comes in time and with patience. The trip is worth the effort.

Over the years there have been many requests for information about carnival glass trademarks and while this section will be old news to seasoned collectors, it may just help beginners avoid costly purchases they will regret. If it saves just one from mistaking reproductions for old carnival, the effort is well worth it.

Northwood, Imperial, Cambridge, Dugan/Diamond, McKee, Higbee, Jeannette, Sowerby (England), and Cristales de Mexico (Mexico) are the trademarks on old glass that collectors will see. All these companies marked at least a part of their production. The dates for marking vary and range from 1904 to 1939, depending on the company's lifespan and when it first started marking glass.

On the other hand, many well-known glassmakers never marked old glass. These include Fenton, Millersburg, U.S. Glass, Fostoria, Indiana, and others. Fostoria and Fenton used paper labels on their products and over the years these have been washed off. Others depended on advertising to identify their products and marked the packaging.

Now let's take a look at the most often seen old glass markings:

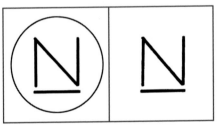

NORTHWOOD

CRISTALES DE MEXICO

DIAMOND
(DUGAN/DIAMOND)

HIGBEE

IMPERIAL

CAMBRIDGE

JEANNETTE

PRES-CUT

McKEE

New Marks

New glass trademarks generally fall into two categories: marks intended to appear close enough to old, well-known trademarks to fool buyers, or completely new trademarks that bear no resemblance to old markings. Here are some of each, all familiar to many carnival glass collectors and dealers. Remember, the old Northwood trademark is owned by the American Carnival Glass Association; the purchasing of this trademark was done to keep it from being copied and the hard work of this organization has stopped many dishonest attempts at copying. The A.C.G.A. has to be commended for its efforts, but as you can see from the first two modern markings, clever attempts to deceive weren't completely stopped. Here are the most often found new marks:

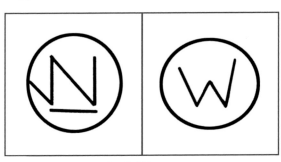

L. G. Wright

This trademark, often found on many patterns that were made in old carnival, is an obvious attempt to fool the buyer into believing the product is old Northwood and has caused great confusion over the years.

Boyd is currently using this mark on many types of glass including carnival as well as making some items that are not marked.

Boyd

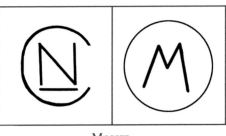

Mosser

Once again, an attempt to deceive the buyer into thinking the product is Northwood. This mark is even more deceptive than the Wright mark and can be found on Northwood patterns that were also made in old glass. Beware! In addition, Mosser has a third mark, consisting of an "M" inside the outline of the state of Ohio. All three marks can be found on new carnival glass as well as other types of glass.

The Fenton Company has been the most responsible glasshouse as far as marking its new glass reproductions. Beginning in 1971 virtually every piece of glass from the Fenton factory has been marked and the company is to be complimented.

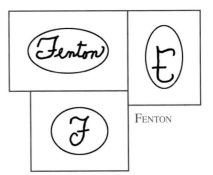

FENTON

SMITH GLASS COMPANY

SUMMIT GLASS COMPANY

The Imperial Company began using its well-known "IG" mark on reissue patterns in 1951 and marked just about all its products until the company's liquidation in 1973 when a large "L" was added. In 1981 Arthur Lorch bought the company and added an "A" to the trademark. In 1982, Mr. Lorch sold the plant to Robert Stahl who declared bankruptcy in 1984 and closed the factory in 1985. Molds were sold and some were purchased by Summit Glass and are still in production. In addition, Rosso Glass of Pennsylvania reproduces glass in carnival and other treatments and its mark is an "R" in a keystone shape.

IMPERIAL
(1951 – 1972)

IMPERIAL GLASS
LIQUIDATION CORP.
(1973 – 1981)

IMPERIAL GLASS
LORCH OWNERSHIP
(1981 – 1982)

11

Many companies are making new carnival from old molds or creating new molds never found in old glass production. The Indiana Glass Company of Dunkirk, Indiana, has revived some of its old patterns and created new ones. Its large production of geometric patterns in red carnival and the copycat version of the Imperial #474 vase in red have caused unexperienced collectors concern for many months, and hardly a week goes by I don't hear from someone who bought these as old glass. Other small concerns are copying old patterns in carnival and opalescent glass without marking them in any way. So please be cautious; buy only what you know is authentic. If a pattern shape or color not listed in this book shows up in a mall booth, it is probably not old. Toothpick holders, table set pieces, and water set pieces seem to be the most copied shapes but there are bowl copies flooding the stands from the East, especially Taiwan and Hong Kong. Many Northwood, Fenton, and other company patterns are among these, so beware!

About Pricing

Pricing carnival glass is a difficult task because one must take into account not only patterns, colors, and shapes but also the quality of the iridescence. Beginning collectors sometimes fail to understand that a price guide cannot reflect individual sales. At the same time, advanced collectors have complicated the mix by concocting new colors or shades of colors that affect prices.

All prices listed are based on extensive research of auction sales, shop taggings, and private sales where information was forthcoming, and some are pure speculation on pieces that seldom change hands.

Mike Carwile
180 Cheyenne Drive
Lynchburg, VA 24502
434-237-4247
e-mail: mcarwile@jetbroadband.com

MADE BY
Fenton, 1920

Plate, rare
Marigold   3,800

— MADE BY
Fenton, 1911

Pitcher
    Marigold   3,000

MADE BY
Fenton, 1910 – 1912

Compote

Marigold	60
Amethyst	85
Green	95
Blue	90

MADE BY
Millersburg, 1911

Compote, rare

Marigold	2,000
Amethyst	2,400
Green	3,100
Vaseline	5,000

Acorn Vase

MADE BY
Millersburg, 1911

Handled, rare

Marigold	2,800
Amethyst	3,300
Green	4,000
Vaseline	5,500

A Dozen Roses

MADE BY

Imperial, 1915?

Bowl, footed, 8" – 10", scarce

Marigold	550
Amethyst	900
Green	800

MADE BY
Czechoslovakian, 1920s

Vase, enameled, 8-sided
Marigold   70

MADE BY
Jain, 1930s?

Pitcher
Marigold   365

Tumbler
Marigold   150

Angoori

MADE BY

Agarwal Glass Works, 1930s?

Tumbler
    Marigold   175

Apple and Pear Intaglio

MADE BY
Northwood, 1914?

Bowl, 5"
    Marigold   60

Bowl, 10"
    Marigold   115

Apple Blossom (Enameled)

MADE BY
Northwood, 1909 – 1912

Pitcher
Blue   475

Tumbler
Blue   90

Apple Panels

MADE BY
Unknown, 1920s?

Creamer

Marigold   35

Sugar (open)

Marigold   35

MADE BY
Fenton, 1920s

Toothpick Holder

Wisteria	150
Celeste Blue	125
Ice Green	125
Vaseline	100

MADE BY

Cristolerias Rigolleau, 1920s?

Inkwell, very rare
Amber 2,700

MADE BY
Unknown, 1920s?

Vase, 7¼"
    Marigold   225

MADE BY
Austrian, 1920s

Bowl, enameled
Blue   850

MADE BY
McKee, 1920s

Pitcher, rare
Marigold 1,300

Tumbler, very scarce
Marigold 650

Creamer
Clambroth 250
Marigold 250

MADE BY
Imperial, 1910

Compote, 4½", scarce
Marigold   60

Banded Rib Neck Vase

MADE BY
Czechoslovakian, 1930s

Vase, with black band
Marigold   75

Band of Roses

MADE BY
European, 1920s?

Pitcher
    Marigold   250

Tumbler
    Marigold   150

Tray
    Marigold   75

Tumble-up, two pieces
    Marigold   200

MADE BY
Westmoreland, 1910

Creamer with lid

Marigold	50
Amethyst	75
Green	100
White	175

Sugar with lid

Marigold	50
Amethyst	75
Green	100
White	175

Syrup whimsey

Marigold	180

MADE BY
Imperial, 1909 – 1910

Milk pitcher

Marigold	300
Green	375
Smoke	175

Beaded Panels

MADE BY
Dugan, 1910 – 1912

REPRODUCTIONS
Yes

Compote

Marigold	60
Amethyst	225
Blue	350
Peach Opalescent	95

MADE BY
Northwood, 1912?

Shade, either
Marigold   75

MADE BY
Northwood, 1908 – 1909

Bowl, 8½"
    Marigold   45
    Amethyst   60
    Green   70

MADE BY
U.S. Glass, 1914 – 1915

Rose bowl, rare

Marigold	350
Clambroth	300

Spooner, rare

Marigold	125

Bernheimer

MADE BY
Millersburg, 1911

Bowl, 8¾", scarce
Blue   2,500

MADE BY
Unknown, 1920?

Mustard with lid
Marigold   700

Big Thistle

MADE BY
Millersburg, 1912

Punch bowl and base, very rare
Amethyst   15,000

ALSO KNOWN AS
Bluebird

MADE BY
Indiana Glass Co., 1915?

Tumbler, very scarce
Marigold   150

ALSO KNOWN AS
Daisy & Plume

MADE BY
Northwood, 1909 – 1913

Candy dish, 3 footed, berry interior

Marigold	90
Amethyst	200
Green	165
Blue	1,500
Ice Blue	750
Ice Green	900
White	500
Lime Green	900

Rose bowl, 3 footed, berry interior

Marigold	100
Amethyst	185
Green	175
Blue	900
Aqua Opalescent	9,000
Ice Blue	1,300
Ice Green	1,150
White	550
Amber	1,000

MADE BY
Fenton, 1911 – 1912

Hat shape

Marigold	35
Amethyst	75
Green	55
Blue	45
Peach Opalescent	135
White	200
Iridized Moonstone	125

Unknown, 1909 – 1912?

Vase, rare
    Amethyst   12,000

MADE BY
Fenton, 1920s

Candy with lid
Marigold   65

MADE BY
U.S. Glass, 1913

Spooner, very scarce
Marigold   150

Block Band Diamond

MADE BY
U. S. Glass, 1915

All pieces scarce to rare and have enameled decoration.

Berry bowl, small		**Spooner**	
Marigold	75	Marigold	90
Berry bowl, large		**Sugar with lid**	
Marigold	125	Marigold	115
Butter		**Syrup, decorated, rare**	
Marigold	300	Marigold	250
Creamer		**Tumbler**	
Marigold	90	Marigold	150

MADE BY
Fenton, 1912

Pitcher, scarce

Marigold	500
Blue	2,000

Tumbler, scarce

Marigold	45
Green	150
Blue	100
White	200

European?, 1920?

Cider pitcher
Marigold   600

Mug
Marigold   160

MADE BY
Millersburg, 1910

Compote

Marigold	100
Amethyst	135
Green	150

Breakfast Set

Indiana, 1912 – 1914?

Creamer
    Marigold   50

Sugar
    Marigold   50

Britt Tumbler

MADE BY
Finland, 1930s

Very rare
Blue   1,000

MADE BY
Fostoria, 1920s?

Bonbon			**Footed center bowl**	
Ice Green	55		Ice Green	225
Bread tray			**Ice bucket**	
Ice Green	185		Ice Green	250
Cake plate			**Planter with frog**	
Ice Green	150		Ice Green	500
Covered box			**Rose bowl**	
Ice Green	225		Ice Green	175
Dome bowl			**Vase**	
Ice Green	85		Ice Green	225

Bubble Waves

MADE BY
Unknown, 1910 – 1920?

Compote, rare
Peach Opalescent   150

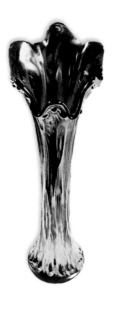

MADE BY
Fenton, 1911

Vase, 14" – 18"
Marigold   125
Blue   150

Bushel Basket

MADE BY
Northwood, 1910 – 1913

Either shape, footed

Marigold	100
Amethyst	90
Green	300
Blue	125
Aqua Opalescent	375
Ice Blue	350
Ice Green	275
White	200
Horehound	350

MADE BY
Millersburg, 1911

Vase, very rare

Marigold	6,500
Amethyst	15,000
Green	16,000
Vaseline	9,000

Buttermilk Goblet

MADE BY
Fenton, 1910 – 1911

Goblet

Marigold	50
Amethyst	75
Green	85
Red	125

Buzz Saw Cruet

MADE BY
Cambridge, 1912

4", scarce
    Green   575

4", with metal tag lettered "B.P.O.E. #1," rare
    Green   1,000

6", scarce
    Marigold   425
    Green   400

MADE BY
Cambridge, 1912

Cruet, rare
Marigold   450

MADE BY
Fenton, 1928

Vase, 11" – 17", scarce
Celeste Blue   250

Camiella Loop

MADE BY
European?, 1920s?

Vase, 5¾"
Marigold   150

Candle Vase

MADE BY
Fenton, 1910 – 1915

One size
   Marigold   55

Cane and Daisy Cut

MADE BY
Jenkins?, 1920s?

Basket, handled, rare
Marigold	220
Smoke	250

Vase
Marigold	150

Argentina, 1930s

Tumbler
Marigold   200

Tumble-Up
Marigold   350

Cannonball Variant

MADE BY
Fenton, 1910

Pitcher

Marigold	240
Blue	285
White	400

Tumbler

Marigold	40
Blue	50
White	75

MADE BY
Heisey, 1915 – 1920?

Bonbon
  Marigold   60

Compote
  Marigold   50

Goblet
  Marigold   75

Channeled Flute

MADE BY
Northwood, 1910 – 1915?

Vase, 10" – 16"

Marigold	65
Amethyst	90
Blue	100
Alaskan	
(Marigold over Green)	150

Cherry Circles

MADE BY
Fenton, 1920

Bonbon

Marigold	45
Amethyst	125
Green	200
Blue	95
Red	4,000
Powder Blue	225

Jefferson, 1915?

Bonbon, small, stemmed
Marigold   35

Bonbon, large, stemmed
Marigold   60

Coal Bucket

MADE BY
U. S. Glass, 1914 – 1915

One size, scarce

Marigold	200
Green	350

Coin Dot Variant

MADE BY
Fenton, 1911 – 1912

Bowl

Marigold	35
Amethyst	45
Green	55
Blue	50

MADE BY
Imperial, 1910

Child's mug, handled
Marigold   65

Lemonade goblet
Marigold   40

Open creamer or sugar
Marigold   30

MADE BY
Imperial, 1909

Compote, scarce
Marigold   75

Compote Vase

MADE BY
Fenton, 1912

Stemmed whimsey

Marigold	50
Amethyst	65
Green	70
Blue	75

MADE BY
Dugan/Diamond, 1910

Vase, very rare
Aqua Opalescent   3,500

Concave Diamonds

MADE BY
Northwood, 1917

Coaster, not iridized
Celeste Blue   65

Pickle caster, complete
Marigold   750
Vaseline   175

Pitcher with lid
Russet Green (Olive)   450
Celeste Blue   300

Tumbler
Russet Green (Olive)   400
Celeste Blue   60

Tumble-up, complete, rare
Olive Green   115
Russet Green (Olive)   155

Vase
Celeste Blue   200

MADE BY
Westmoreland, 1910

Banana bowl

Marigold	65
Amethyst	85
Amber	100

Bowl

Marigold	45
Amethyst	55
Green	65
Teal	75

Plate, 8½" – 9", rare

Amethyst	135

Rose bowl

Marigold	60
Amethyst	95
Green	100

Vase

Marigold	40
Amethyst	65
Green	65
Iridized Moonstone	90

Connie

MADE BY
Northwood, 1909 – 1912

Pitcher
    White   750

Tumbler
    White   150

Corinth

MADE BY
Westmoreland, 1910

Bowl

Marigold	40
Amethyst	60
Teal	75

Lamp, rare

Amethyst	250

Vase

Marigold	30
Amethyst	50
Green	75
Peach Opalescent	150
Blue Opalescent	550

Corn Cruet

MADE BY
Unknown, 1914?

One size, rare
White   1,100

MADE BY
Corning, 1920

Insulator, various shapes
Marigold   35+

Covered Frog

MADE BY

Co-Operative Flint Glass Co., 1930?

One size
Marigold	375
Amethyst	450
Green	500
Blue	275
Ice Green	325

Crackle

MADE BY
Jeannette, 1930s

Auto vase
　　Marigold　　　　25

Bowl, 8"
　　Marigold　　　　25

Cut Grecian Gold

MADE BY
Fenton, 1920s

Lamp font
Marigold   100

Dahlia

MADE BY
Jenkins, 1920s

REPRODUCTIONS
Yes

Compote, very scarce
    Marigold   150

Vase, 10", rare
    Marigold   200

MADE BY
Fenton, 1910 – 1912?

Bonbon, scarce

Marigold	125
Blue	200

MADE BY
U. S. Glass, 1914 – 1915

Creamer
Marigold   55

Sugar
Marigold   55

MADE BY
Fenton, 1920s

Vase, rare
Marigold   12,000

Dandelion

MADE BY
Northwood, 1911 – 1912

Mug

Marigold	125
Amethyst	200
Green	550
Blue	325
Aqua Opalescent	750
Blue Opalescent	750

Pitcher

Marigold	475
Amethyst	650
Green	1,200
Ice Blue	7,000
Ice Green	30,000
White	7,500

Mug (Knights Templar), rare

Marigold	300
Ice Blue	650
Ice Green	800

Tumbler

Marigold	45
Amethyst	70
Green	105
Ice Blue	135
Ice Green	300
White	125
Lavender	245

Vase whimsey, rare

Amethyst	850

MADE BY
Imperial, 1909 – 1915

Pair
Marigold   150

Diamond and Bows

MADE BY
Indiana, 1930s

Tumbler
Marigold   200

MADE BY
Imperial, 1909 – 1915

Light shade
Marigold   65

Diamond Points Variant

MADE BY
Fostoria, 1920s

Rose bowl, rare
Marigold   1,200

MADE BY
U. S. Glass, 1914 – 1915

Vase, very rare
Marigold   250

MADE BY
Diamond, 1920s

Candlesticks, pair
Marigold	80
Amethyst	125
Blue	175
Ice Green	125
Red	300

Console bowl
Marigold	55
Amethyst	70
Blue	85
Ice Green	60
Red	135

MADE BY
Sweden, 1930s

Vase, 5¼", rare
Amethyst   350

Double Scroll

MADE BY
Imperial, 1915 – 1920

Bowl, console
Marigold	50
Red	250
Teal	525

Candlesticks, pair
Marigold	75
Red	400
Amberina	300

MADE BY
Diamond, 1910 – 1915

Candy jar, footed, with lid
Marigold 55
Green 75
Blue 85

MADE BY
Dugan, 1909 – 1910

Vase

Marigold	75
Peach Opalescent	175

MADE BY
Dugan, 1910

Hat shape

Marigold	30
Amethyst	40
Blue	75
Peach Opalescent	95

Vase

Marigold	60
Amethyst	80
Blue	75
Peach Opalescent	125

MADE BY
Dugan, 1912

Vase, 8" – 13"
Marigold   50
Amethyst   75
Peach Oplaescent   85

MADE BY
Dugan, 1910

Either shape
| Amethyst | 90 |
| Blue | 110 |

MADE BY
Dugan, 1910

Bowl, footed, 8½"

Marigold	85
Amethyst	175
Green	250
Blue	200
Celeste Blue	900

Plate

Marigold	300
Amethyst	575

MADE BY
Unknown, 1912 – 1914?

Pitcher, enameled, rare
    Marigold   800

Tumbler, enameled, rare
    Marigold   350

MADE BY
Fenton, 1910 – 1915

Pitcher

Marigold	140
Blue	195

Tumbler

Marigold	25
Blue	40

MADE BY
Fenton, 1912 – 1916

Pitcher

Marigold	250
Amethyst	325
Green	350
Blue	450

Tumbler

Marigold	30
Amethyst	40
Green	55
Blue	60

Enameled Double Daisy

MADE BY
Fenton, 1912 – 1916

Pitcher
Marigold	130
Blue	165
White	170

Tumbler
Marigold	20
Blue	30
White	30

Enameled Prism Band

MADE BY
Fenton, 1912 – 1916

Pitcher

Marigold	200
Amethyst	350
Green	375
Blue	300
Ice Green	450
White	365

Tumbler

Marigold	45
Amethyst	55
Green	65
Blue	55
Ice Green	85
White	55

Enameled Swallow

MADE BY
Czechoslovakian, 1930s?

Tankard pitcher with lid
    Marigold   225

Tumbler
    Marigold   50

MADE BY
Imperial, 1909

Compote
Marigold	120
Green	175

Fan Montage

MADE BY
Unknown, 1920s?

Biscuit jar with lid, rare
Marigold   225

Fenton Flute

MADE BY
Fenton, 1911 – 1913

Vase

Marigold	25
Amethyst	55
Green	65
Blue	50
White	90
Red	300
Vaseline	100

MADE BY
Fenton, 1915

Creamer
   Marigold   45

Sugar, open
   Marigold   45

MADE BY
Fenton, 1915

Candlesticks, pair
Marigold	40
Celeste Blue	110

Fenton's #643

MADE BY
Fenton, 1917

Compote
    Marigold   50
    Celeste Blue   70

Covered candy
    Marigold   70
    Celeste Blue   95

Plate, 7"
    Marigold   35
    Ice Green   40

Salver
    Marigold   65
    Ice Green   75

MADE BY
Fenton, 1926

Bowl
    White   65

Candy jar
    Aqua   125

Fan vase
    Ice Green   85

MADE BY
Fenton, 1910 – 1914

Bowl, 5" – 6"

Marigold	25
Amethyst	35
Green	40
Blue	45
Ice Green	55

Bowl, tricornered, 6½"

Marigold	30
Amethyst	45
Green	50
Blue	55
Ice Green	70

Bowl, square, 9", scarce

Marigold	70
Green	90

MADE BY
Fenton, 1910 – 1912

Hat

Marigold	45
Green	60
Blue	50
Red	425

Fine Cut Flowers

MADE BY
Fenton, 1914 – 1916?

Compote
> Marigold   65
> Green   125

Goblet
> Marigold   75
> Green   125

MADE BY
Unknown, 1920s?

3½"

Marigold   90

Floral Oval

MADE BY
Higbee, 1920s?

Bowl, 7"
Marigold   50

Creamer
Marigold   60

Goblet
Marigold   75

Plate, 7", rare
Marigold   90

Florentine

MADE BY
Fenton and Northwood, 1915 – 1918

REPRODUCTIONS
Yes

Candlesticks, large, pair

Marigold	125
Russet Green	160
Blue	700
Ice Green	125
Red	1,100

Candlesticks, small, pair

Marigold	75
Green	120
Blue	450
Red	900
Celeste Blue	110

Flower Medallion

MADE BY
Indiana, 1917?

Tumbler, rare
Marigold   400

MADE BY
Millersburg, 1912

Compote, 6", marked "Krystol," rare
Marigold	500
Amethyst	600

Vase, rare
Marigold	450
Amethyst	600
Green	800
Blue	3,000

Flute (Northwood)

MADE BY
Northwood, 1909 – 1912?

Bowl, 5"
Marigold	25
Amethyst	30

Bowl, 9"
Marigold	45
Amethyst	55

Bowl, 3-in-1 edge, rare
Green	150

Butter
Marigold	135
Green	185

Celery vase
Marigold	75

Creamer
Marigold	75
Green	95

Individual salt, footed
Marigold	35
Vaseline	50

Master salt, footed
Marigold	75
Vaseline	150

Pitcher, rare
Marigold	400
Amethyst	700
Green	600

Plate, very scarce
Marigold	300

Ringtree, rare
Marigold	175

Rose bowl, rare
Marigold	300

Sherbet
Marigold	35
Amethyst	50
Green	45
Teal	80

Sugar
Marigold	75
Green	95

Tumbler, 3 varieties
Marigold	50
Green	300

MADE BY
Imperial, 1909

Bowl, 5½", rare

Marigold	60
Amethyst	75
Green	75

Bowl, 10", rare

Marigold	80
Amethyst	150
Green	150

Bowl, fruit, 11", rare

Marigold	95
Amethyst	175
Green	175

Punch bowl with base, scarce

Marigold	300
Amethyst	500
Green	500

Punch cup, scarce

Marigold	35
Amethyst	50
Green	50

Flute Variant

MADE BY
Northwood, 1910 – 1912

Bowl, 8"
    Marigold   75
    Green   90

MADE BY
Riihimaki, 1939

Candlesticks, pair
Pink   250

MADE BY
Fostoria, 1920?

Spooner
Marigold   75

Four Pillars with Drapes

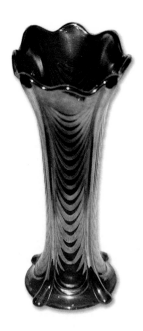

MADE BY
Northwood, 1910 – 1918?

Vase, very scarce
Marigold	100
Green	325
Blue	425
Sapphire Blue	575

Freefold

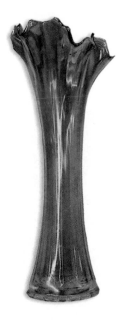

MADE BY
Imperial, 1909 – 1915

Vase, 7" – 14"

Marigold	30
Amethyst	55
Green	45
White	70
Smoke	115

Freesia

MADE BY
Fenton, 1912 – 1916

Pitcher
    Marigold   225

Tumbler
    Marigold   35

Frolicking Bears

MADE BY
U. S. Glass?, 1914 – 1915

Pitcher, very rare
    Green   45,000

Tumbler, very rare
    Green   13,500

Fruit Basket

MADE BY

Millersburg, 1912

Compote, handled, rare

Amethyst   1,600

MADE BY
Indiana, 1920s

Butter
    Marigold   165

Creamer
    Marigold   60

Spooner
    Marigold   60

Sugar with lid
    Marigold   85

Goddess of Harvest

MADE BY
Fenton, 1909

Bowl, 9½", very rare
Marigold	6,000
Amethyst	7,000
Blue	6,500

Plate, very rare
Amethyst	10,000

Golden Bird

MADE BY
Dugan/Diamond, 1911 – 1912?

Nappy, footed, handled
Marigold   300

MADE BY
Unknown, 1924

Bottle, four sizes
Marigold   20 – 75

Gooseberry Spray

MADE BY

U. S. Glass, 1914 – 1916

Bowl, 5", scarce

Marigold	75
Amber	110
Honey Amber	225

Bowl, 5½", tricornered, rare

Marigold	150
White	375
Honey Amber	225

Bowl, 10", scarce

Marigold	65
Amber	95
White	200
Honey Amber	165

Compote, rare

Amber	225
White	300

Rose bowl, 4½", rare

Marigold	125
Honey Amber	325

Imperial, 1901 – 1915?

Vase, 8" – 12", rare

Marigold	125
Smoke	400

Grape and Cable Banded

MADE BY
Northwood, 1910 – 1914

REPRODUCTIONS
Yes

Banana bowl
Marigold 275
Blue 600
Renniger Blue 650

Dresser tray
Marigold 135

Hatpin holder
Marigold 250
Amethyst 450
Blue 700

Orange bowl
Marigold 425
Blue 650
Iridized Custard 3,000

MADE BY
Northwood, 1910 – 1914

Bowl, 6" – 8"

Marigold	65
Amethyst	75
Green	90
Blue	145
Aqua Oplaescent	3,900
Ice Blue	900
Emerald Green	325

Plate, 7½" – 9", scarce

Marigold	135
Amethyst	250
Green	650
Blue	550
Emerald Green	1,200

Plate, handgrip, scarce

Marigold	165
Amethyst	190
Green	245
Blue	500
Lavender	325

Plate, two sides up, 6" – 7½", scarce

Marigold	125
Amethyst	200

(stippled pieces, add 25%)

Grape and Cherry

MADE BY
Unknown, 1920s?

Bowl, 8½", rare
    Marigold   100
    Blue   200

Grape Arbor

MADE BY
Northwood, 1910 – 1914

Hat

Marigold	60
Amethyst	100
Blue	145
Ice Blue	225
Ice Green	325
White	110

Pitcher

Marigold	325
Amethyst	625
Blue	14,000
Ice Blue	1,300
Ice Green	10,000
White	425

Tumbler

Marigold	45
Amethyst	100
Blue	400
Ice Blue	160
Ice Green	325
White	70
Lavender	140

Tumbler (etched)

Amethyst	450
Blue	575
White	75

MADE BY
Northwood, 1909 – 1910

Bowl, 8½", ruffled or 3-in-1 edge

Marigold	45
Amethyst	95
Green	85
Blue	150
Ice Blue	1,400
Amber	225

Bride's basket, complete

Amethyst	300

Hammered Bell

MADE BY
Unknown, 1913?

Chandeliere, complete, five shades
White   600

Shade, each
White   75

MADE BY
Imperial, 1909 – 1915?

Three shapes
Marigold	45
Smoke	90

Candle bowl, scarce
Marigold	110
Amethyst	500

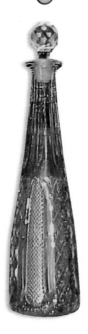

MADE BY
Tarentum, 1920s

Decanter with stopper, 11½"
Marigold   250

MADE BY
Diamond, 1914 – 1915

Pitcher, rare
    Marigold   2,800

Tumbler, very scarce
    Marigold   200
    Amethyst   900
    Green   1,100

Headdress

MADE BY
U. S. Glass, 1914 – 1915

Bowl, 7" – 10"
| | |
Marigold 175
Blue 225

Compote
Marigold 80
Blue 125

MADE BY
Fenton, 1910 – 1914

Plate, 9", scarce
Marigold   800
Blue   1,000

MADE BY
Unknown, 1930?

Lamp
　　Marigold　　　　　450

MADE BY
Australian, 1920s

Bowl, 5"
Marigold	50
Amethyst	75

Bowl, 9"
Marigold	100
Amethyst	125

MADE BY
Imperial, 1909 – 1915

Bowl, 10"
    Marigold   45

Compote
    Marigold   45
    Green   55

Creamer
    Marigold   30

Sugar
    Marigold   35

Vase
    Marigold   50
    Green   65
    Smoke   85

Heavy Web

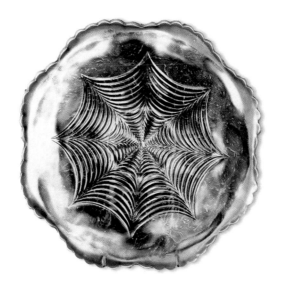

MADE BY
Dugan, 1920

Bowl, 10", very scarce
    Peach Opalescent   700

Plate, 11", rare
    Peach Opalescent   3,500

MADE BY
Heisey, 1920s – 1930s

Spittoon
Marigold   150

MADE BY
Heisey, 1920s – 1930s

Punch cup
Marigold   35

Toothpick holder
Marigold   150

MADE BY
Heisey, 1924

Bowl, footed, 11", rare
Marigold   300

ALSO KNOWN AS
#341

MADE BY
Heisey, 1915 – 1920?

Compote

Marigold	75
Amethyst	200
Vaseline	150

Compote, tricornered whimsey

Marigold	125

Heron Mug

MADE BY

Dugan, 1910

Rare

Marigold	1,500
Amethyst	125

MADE BY
Imperial, 1910

Compote, rare
Marigold   200

MADE BY
Unknown, 1920s

Child's breakfast set, complete
Lavender   60

MADE BY
McKee-Federal, 1914

Banana bowl whimsey, very rare
Marigold   150

Caster set, four pieces
Marigold   325
Pastel Marigold   450

MADE BY
Northwood, 1912 – 1915?

Tray, 11", scarce
Marigold   225

MADE BY
Dugan, 1910 – 1912

Compote, very rare
Marigold   5,000

MADE BY
Czechoslovakian? 1930s?

Lamp shade
Marigold   65

MADE BY
Millersburg, 1910

Vase, 8¼", rare
Amethyst	7,300
Blue	8,200

MADE BY
Fenton, 1920s

Bowl, 8", scarce
Marigold   50

Rose bowl, low, 6½"
Marigold   75

MADE BY
Consolidated, 1914 – 1915

Rare
Caramel   4,000

Idyll

MADE BY
Fenton, 1911

Vase, very rare
Marigold	650
Amethyst	800
Blue	900

MADE BY
Imperial, 1920s

Fruit bowl, 9", handled
Marigold	75
Smoke	125

Tray, 10", handled
Marigold	65
Smoke	100

Imperial #499

Imperial, 1920s

Sherbet

Marigold	15
Green	30
Red	95

MADE BY
Imperial, 1920s

Tray, center handle
Smoke   65

Imperial Flute Vase

MADE BY

Imperial, 1909 – 1915

Vase with serrated top

Marigold	40
Amethyst	80
Green	65
Blue	500

MADE BY
Imperial, 1909 – 1915

Advertising weight, very rare
Amethyst   1,200

MADE BY

Diamond, 1915 – 1918?

Bowl, 4½"
    Marigold   30
    Amethyst   90

Bowl, 7½"
    Marigold   50
    Amethyst   150

MADE BY

Unknown, 1920s?

Tumbler, rare

Marigold   150

MADE BY
U. S. Glass, 1914 – 1915

Rose bowl
Marigold   85

Jester's Cap

MADE BY
Westmoreland, 1910

Vase

Marigold	75
Amber	100
Green	100
Peach Opalescent	200
Blue Opalescent	300
Teal	150

Jewels

MADE BY
Diamond, 1916 – 1918?

Bowl, various sizes

Amethyst	50
Green	150
Blue	175
Red	200
Celeste Blue	80

Candle bowl

Marigold	85
White	175

Candlesticks, pair

Marigold	100
Amethyst	150
Green	175
Blue	200
Red	275
Celeste Blue	150

Vase

Marigold	75
Amethyst	150
Green	150
Blue	175
Red	200
Amber	200

MADE BY
Unknown, 1915 – 1920?

Bowl, 8" – 9", scarce
Marigold   55

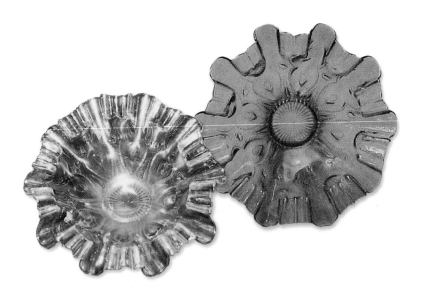

MADE BY
Dugan, 1910 – 1912

Bowl, 9½", very scarce

Marigold	300
Amethyst	375
Peach Opalescent	350

Ladders

Imperial, 1909 – 1915

Bowl, 8", very scarce
Marigold   100

MADE BY
Brockwitz, 1931

Vase, 9½"
    Marigold   275
    Blue   300

MADE BY
Dugan, 1910 – 1912

Vase

Marigold	40
Amethyst	95
Blue	225
Peach Opalescent	175
White	100

MADE BY
Fenton, 1912

Pitcher, rare
Blue   7,000

Tumbler, rare
Marigold   525
Blue   225

Long Buttress

MADE BY
Fostoria, 1910 – 1915

Pitcher
    Marigold   400

Tumbler
    Marigold   250

Toothpick
    Marigold   200

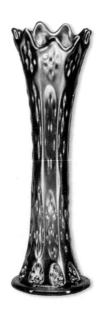

MADE BY
Fenton, 1910 – 1914

Vase, 7" – 11"

Marigold	50
Amethyst	65
Green	75
Blue	130

Louisa

MADE BY
Westmoreland, 1930s

Bowl, footed
Amethyst	95
Green	75
Peach Opalescent	135
Aqua	65

Candy dish, footed
Marigold	50
Amethyst	85
Green	65
Aqua	70

Mini banana boat
Marigold	45
Amethyst	70

Nut bowl, scarce
Amethyst	250

Plate, footed, 8", rare
Marigold	100
Amethyst	165
Peach Opalescent	350
Aqua	125

Rose bowl
Marigold	50
Amethyst	70
Green	65
Blue	175
Teal	75

MADE BY

Fenton, 1911

Scarce

Marigold	225
Amethyst	700
Green	400
Blue	325
Peach Opalescent	7,000
Aqua Opalescent	15,000
White	550

MADE BY
Imperial, 1915?

Bowl, 4", rare
Marigold   65

Bowl, 8¾", rare
Marigold   135

Lutz Mug

MADE BY
McKee, 1920s

Footed
    Marigold   100

MADE BY
McKee, 1920s

Tumbler, rare
Marigold   500

MADE BY
U. S. Glass, 1914 – 1915

Decanter
Marigold   250

Wine
Marigold   40

Vase, rare
Marigold   350

Model Flint Glass Co., 1912?

Vase, 8", very rare
Aqua Opalescent   3,000

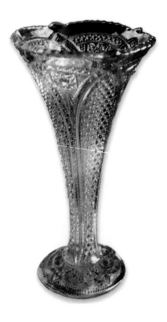

MADE BY
U. S. Glass, 1914 – 1915

Mug, rare
Marigold   150

Tumbler, very scarce
Marigold   200

Vase, very scarce
Marigold   175

MADE BY
Millersburg, 1910

Bowl, 8½" – 10"
Marigold	3,500
Green	150

MADE BY
McKee, 1927

Sherbet
Marigold   35

Miniature Blackberry

MADE BY
Fenton, 1910 – 1912

Compote, small
Marigold	80
Amethyst	125
Green	200
Blue	75
White	525

Stemmed plate, very scarce
Blue	450
White	450

MADE BY
Millersburg, 1910

Vase, rare

Marigold	9,000
Amethyst	10,000
Green	8,000

MADE BY
European, 1930s

Powder jar with lid
Marigold   125

MADE BY
Northwood, 1906

Compote
Marigold	100
Amethyst	150
Green	200

Goblet, rare
Marigold	175
Amethyst	125

Pitcher, rare
Marigold	3,500

Tumbler, rare
Marigold	300
Amethyst	1,200

Northwood #637

MADE BY
Northwood, 1915 – 1918

Compote, either shape
Celeste Blue   125

MADE BY

Northwood, 1915 – 1918

Candlesticks, two sizes

Green	100
Blue	135
Vaseline	150

Northwood Swirl

MADE BY
Northwood, 1910 – 1912

Pitcher
    Marigold   225
    Green   700

Pitcher, #2 Variant
    Marigold   250

Tumbler
    Marigold   75
    Green   125

Whimsey pitcher, no handle
    Marigold   300

MADE BY
Westmoreland, 1910

REPRODUCTIONS
Yes

Compote

Marigold	50
Amethyst	90
Russet Green (Olive)	140
Marigold Milk Glass	100
Blue Opalescent	150
Aqua	150

Open Edge Basketweave

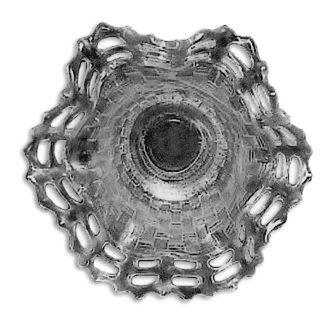

MADE BY
Fenton, 1911

Bowl, small, either shape
Marigold	30
Amethyst	150
Green	150
Blue	50
White	160
Red	325
Smoke	150

Bowl, large, either shape
Marigold	75
Amethyst	175
Green	175
Blue	70
Ice Blue	300
Ice Green	375
White	190
Celeste Blue	450

REPRODUCTIONS
Yes

Bowl, square, scarce
Marigold	50
Amethyst	160
Green	250
Blue	80
Red	600
Aqua	115

Bowl, tricornered, scarce
Blue	200

Hat, JIP shape
Marigold	25
Amethyst	125
Green	180
Blue	40
White	125
Red	375
Aqua	225

Plate, rare
Marigold	900
Blue	1,400
Ice Blue	1,900
White	625

Vase whimsey, rare
Marigold	800
Green	1,200
Red	3,000

MADE BY

Imperial, 1909 – 1915

Bowls, 5" – 8"
Marigold	30
Clambroth	40

Bowl, handled, 12"
Marigold	45
Clambroth	50

Cup and saucer, rare
Marigold	300
Clambroth	250

Goblet
Marigold	60
Lavender	90

Plate, 10½"
Marigold	70
Clambroth	75

Pitcher, small, rare
Marigold	185
Clambroth	200

Tumbler, two shapes
Marigold	50
Clambroth	40

Rose bowl
Marigold	90
Clambroth	75

Salt cup, rare
Marigold	200

MADE BY
Imperial, 1909 – 1915

Bowl, 5"
    Marigold   20
    Smoke   35

Bowl, 10"
    Marigold   35
    Smoke   50

Compote
    Marigold   50
    Clambroth   60

Plate, 8", rare
    Clambroth   200

Spittoon whimsey, scarce
    Marigold   225

Orange Peel

MADE BY
Westmoreland, 1912 – 1914

Custard cup, scarce
Marigold	25

Dessert, stemmed, scarce
Marigold	45
Amethyst	70
Russet Green	80
Teal	70

Punch bowl with base
Marigold	200
Amethyst	250
Teal	250

Punch cup
Marigold	10
Amethyst	40
Teal	35

MADE BY
Fenton, 1914

Pitcher
Marigold	475
Blue	900

Tumbler
Marigold	50
Blue	75

MADE BY
Fenton, 1911

Pitcher
Marigold	400
Blue	600
White	425

Tumbler
Marigold	35
Blue	85
White	125

Whimsey, handled, from pitcher, rare
Marigold	7,000

MADE BY
Fenton, 1910

Vase, 5" – 12"

Marigold	75
Amethyst	125
Green	160
Blue	95

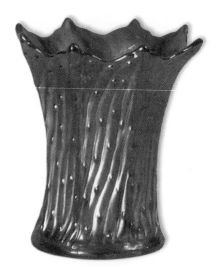

MADE BY
Dugan, 1910

Vase, 7" – 12", rare
Amethyst   5,250

Petals

MADE BY
Northwood, 1909 – 1912

Compote

Marigold	50
Amethyst	65
Green	150
Blue	1,000
Ice Blue	900

MADE BY
Dugan, 1910

Vase

Marigold	85
Peach Opalescent	180

Plain Jane

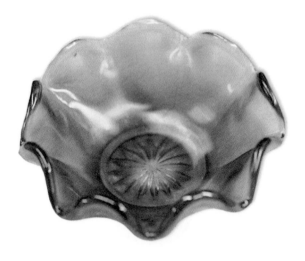

MADE BY
Imperial, 1909

Basket

Marigold	30
Amethyst	125
Ice Green	200
Smoke	65

Bowl, 4"

Marigold	15
Amethyst	50
Green	35
Smoke	25

Bowl, 4", smooth edge

Marigold	25
Powder Blue	55

Bowl, 8" – 9"

Marigold	40
Amethyst	75
Green	45
Smoke	65

Bowl, 10" – 12"

Marigold	60
Amethyst	100
Green	70
Smoke	100

Rose bowl, small

Marigold	45
Smoke	75

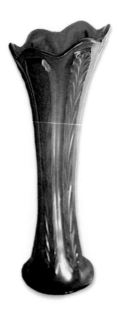

MADE BY
Fenton, 1912

Vase, 7" – 12"

Marigold	30
Amethyst	100
Green	225
Blue	165
Red	1,300
Vaseline	500

Vase, JIP, rare

Red	1,400

Poppy Variant

MADE BY
Northwood, 1909 – 1912?

Bowl, 7" – 8"

Marigold	50
Amethyst	75
Green	80
Blue	175
Peach Oplaescent	350
Aqua Opalescent	595
Alaskan (Marigold over Green)	85

MADE BY
U. S. Glass, 1914 – 1915

Bowl, 5"
Marigold   95

Bowl, 8"
Marigold   170

Toothpick holder
Marigold   140

Wine
Marigold   165

Pressed Hexagon

MADE BY
McKee, 1920s

Covered butter
  Marigold   150

Creamer
  Marigold   85

Spooner
  Marigold   85

Sugar
  Marigold   85

MADE BY
Fenton, 1912 – 1916

Pitcher

Marigold	200
Blue	300
Ice Green	450

Tumbler

Marigold	30
Blue	45
Ice Green	100

Pulled Loop

MADE BY
Dugan/Diamond, 1920s

Vase, squat, 5" – 7"

Marigold	80
Amethyst	175
Peach Opalescent	300
White	385
Celeste Blue	750

Vase, 8" – 16"

Marigold	40
Amethyst	75
Green	300
Blue	175
Peach Opalescent	250
Celeste Blue	950

Rainbow

MADE BY
Northwood, 1910 – 1912

Bowl, 8"
Marigold	45
Amethyst	65
Green	75
Lavender	125

Compote
Marigold	45
Amethyst	65
Green	80

Plate, 9", scarce
Amethyst	100
Green	150

Plate, handgrip, 9", scarce
Amethyst	150
Green	175

MADE BY
Brockwitz, 1931

Tumbler, rare
Marigold   700

MADE BY
Unknown, 1915?

Bowl, rare

Marigold	1,900
Green	2,200

MADE BY
Northwood, 1910

Bowl, footed, 7" – 9"

Marigold	60
Amethyst	100
Green	165

MADE BY

Heisey, 1912?

Tumbler, rare
    Marigold   250

Pitcher
    Marigold   375

Scroll Fluted

MADE BY
Imperial, 1910?

Rose bowl, very rare
Marigold   325

MADE BY
Fenton, 1912 – 1916

Pitcher

Marigold	250
Ice Green	425
White	375

Tumbler

Marigold	35
Ice Green	55
White	40

MADE BY

Imperial, 1909 – 1915

Bowl, 7" – 9"

Marigold	125
Amethyst	250
Green	100
Smoke	225

Plate, 9"

Marigold	800
Amethyst	1,500
Green	275
Smoke	900

Shrine Champagne

ALSO KNOWN AS
Rochester

MADE BY
U. S. Glass, 1914 – 1915

Clear   100

Simple Simon

MADE BY
Northwood, 1909 – 1910

Vase

Marigold	60
Amethyst	75
Green	90

MADE BY
Westmoreland, 1915 – 1920

Toothpick holder
Smoke   350

MADE BY
Imperial, 1909 – 1915

Bowl, 9" – 10"
Marigold	25
Smoke	20

Champagne
Marigold	40
Smoke	40

Custard cup
Marigold	15
Smoke	15

Goblet, two sizes
Marigold	30
Smoke	30

Plate, 8"
Marigold	35
Smoke	40

Plate, 12"
Marigold	50
Smoke	55

Pitcher
Marigold	65
Smoke	75

Rose bowl
Marigold	80

Tumbler
Marigold	20
Smoke	25

Wine, two sizes
Marigold	35
Smoke	40

MADE BY
Northwood, 1909 – 1910

Bonbon

Marigold	35
Amethyst	45
Green	55
Alaskan (Marigold over Green)	60

Bowl, 6" – 7"

Marigold	30
Amethyst	40
Green	45
Blue	750

Compote

Marigold	40
Amethyst	45
Green	55

MADE BY
Cambridge, 1915?

Tankard, very rare
Marigold   2,000

MADE BY

Dugan, 1910

Bowl, 10", scarce
Peach Opalescent   200

Plate, 10½", rare
Peach Opalescent   350

Lamp, complete, scarce
Marigold   350

MADE BY
Fenton, 1916

Fan vase
Marigold   95

MADE BY
U. S. Glass?, 1915?

Vase, 6"
Marigold 90

S-Repeat

MADE BY
Dugan, 1910

REPRODUCTIONS
Yes

Creamer, small
Amethyst   75

Creamer whimsey (from punch cup)
Amethyst   100

Punch bowl with base, rare
Amethyst   4,800

Punch cup, rare
Amethyst   100

Sugar, rare (very light iridescence)
Amethyst   250

Toothpick holder (old only, rare)
Amethyst   90

Tumbler
Marigold   475
Amethyst   125

MADE BY
Unknown, 1915 – 1920?

Vase, 5½"
　　Marigold　　　　　50

Stippled Mum

MADE BY
Northwood, 1910 – 1912?

Bowl, 9", scarce

Marigold	75
Amethyst	150
Green	165
Blue	200

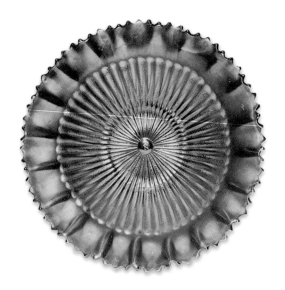

MADE BY
Northwood, 1909

Bonbon

Marigold	35
Amethyst	40
Green	45
Blue	90

Bowl, 8" – 10"

Marigold	40
Amethyst	55
Green	60
Blue	170
White	125
Aqua	225

Bowl, 11", very scarce

Amethyst	100

Compote

Marigold	50
Amethyst	60
Green	65

Rose bowl, very rare

Amethyst	950

Stork and Rushes

Basket, handled

Marigold	125

Bowl, 5"

Marigold	30
Amethyst	30

Bowl, 10"

Marigold	40
Amethyst	50

Butter, rare

Marigold	150
Amethyst	175

Creamer, rare

Marigold	80
Amethyst	90

Hat

Marigold	25
Amethyst	75
Blue	30

MADE BY
Dugan, 1910

REPRODUCTIONS
Yes

Mug

Marigold	25
Amethyst	175
Blue	1,000
Aqua	650

Pitcher

Marigold	250
Amethyst	225
Blue	500

Punch bowl with base, rare

Marigold	200
Amethyst	300
Blue	350

Punch cup

Marigold	20
Amethyst	30
Blue	35

Spooner, rare

Marigold	80
Amethyst	90

Sugar, rare

Marigold	90
Amethyst	120

Tumbler

Marigold	30
Amethyst	60
Blue	75

MADE BY
Dugan/Diamond, 1910 – 1915

Epergne, rare
Amethyst   900

MADE BY
Fenton, 1910 – 1915

Bonbon

Marigold	50
Amethyst	75
Green	90
Blue	140
Red	450
Lime Opalescent	375

MADE BY
Northwood, 1908

Bowl, 5½"
    Marigold   30

Bowl, 9½"
    Marigold   65

MADE BY
Fenton, 1912

Pitcher, rare
Marigold	3,500
Blue	3,000

Tumbler, rare
Marigold	160
Blue	135

MADE BY
Millersburg, 1910

Banana boat whimsey, rare
Amethyst	2,000
Green	2,000
Vaseline	2,600

Bowl, 6½" – 7½"
Marigold	75
Amethyst	150
Green	200
Vaseline	1,800

Bowl, 8" – 10", scarce
Marigold	185
Amethyst	275
Green	300
Vaseline	1,500

Bowl, 9", square
Marigold	325
Amethyst	400
Green	425

Bowl, tricornered, 9½"
Marigold	450
Amethyst	650
Green	750

Compote, scarce
Marigold	350
Amethyst	300
Green	400

Gravy boat whimsey, rare
Vaseline	3,000

Superb Drape

MADE BY
Unknown, 1910 – 1920?

Vase, very rare
Marigold	2,500
Green	3,500
Aqua Opalescent	5,000

MADE BY
Imperial, 1909 – 1915

Bowl
    Marigold   40

Candlesticks, each
    Marigold   35

Mug, rare
    Marigold   90

Plate
    Marigold   80

Vase
    Marigold   40

MADE BY
U. S. Glass, 1914 – 1915

Spooner, rare
Marigold   250

Target Vase

MADE BY
Dugan/Diamond, 1910 – 1915

Vase, 5" – 7"

Marigold	40
Amethyst	250
Blue	225
Peach Opalescent	140
White	150
Iridized Moonstone	100

Vase, 8" – 13"

Marigold	25
Amethyst	175
Green	425
Blue	175
Peach Opalescent	65
Vaseline	400

MADE BY
U. S. Glass, 1913 – 1914

Breakfast creamer or sugar, each
Lavender   75

MADE BY
Imperial?, 1910 – 1920?

Vase, 4" – 11"

Marigold	125
Amethyst	225
Green	200
Blue	900

MADE BY

Dugan/Diamond, 1910 – 1915

Candy with lid, two sizes

Marigold	75
Ice Green	125
Red	275

Goblet

Marigold	50
Blue	125
Ice Green	85
Red	165

Three Diamonds

Argentina, 1930s

Tumble-up, three pieces
Marigold	175

Vase, 6" – 10"
Marigold	45
Amethyst	50
Green	60
Blue	75
Peach Opalescent	75
Clambroth	60

MADE BY
Imperial, 1909 – 1915

Vase, rare

Marigold	2,400
Amethyst	2,900
Smoke	4,500

MADE BY
McKee, 1920s

Butter, rare
Ruby Iridescent   375

Pitcher, tankard, very rare
Marigold   2,600

Tulip and Cane

MADE BY
Imperial, 1909

Bowl
    Marigold   35

Claret goblet, rare
    Marigold   175

Goblet, 8 oz., rare
    Marigold   100

Jelly compote, ruffled, 5", rare
    Marigold   150

Nappy, handled, rare
    Marigold   200

Wine, two sizes, rare
    Marigold   85

MADE BY

Diamond, 1915

Tall vase

Marigold	30
Amethyst	70

Squat vase, very scarce

Marigold	300
Amethyst	1,100
Aqua Opalescent	2,300

Valentine

MADE BY

Northwood, 1910

Bowl, 5", scarce

Marigold	100
Amethyst	225

Bowl, 10", scarce

Marigold	400

Vining Twigs

MADE BY

Dugan/Diamond, 1910 – 1915

Bowl, 7½"

Marigold	35
Amethyst	45
Green	50

Hat

Marigold	40
Amethyst	50
White	65

Plate, 7", rare

White	425
Lavender	300

MADE BY
Millersburg, 1911

Bowl, 5", rare

Marigold	800
Green	1,100
Blue	2,500

Bowl, 9", rare

Marigold	700
Amethyst	950
Green	825
Blue	400

MADE BY
Northwood, 1910

Bowl, 8" – 9"

Marigold	60
Amethyst	75
Green	90
Black Amethyst	100

MADE BY
Unknown, 1910 – 1915?

Either type

Marigold	40
Amethyst	50
Blue	95

MADE BY
Fostoria, 1920s

Toothpick holder, scarce
Marigold   250

MADE BY
Westmoreland, 1920s

Basket, small
Marigold   25

Basket, large
Marigold   45

MADE BY
Westmoreland, 1910 – 1912

Compote, tall, stemmed
Amethyst   95

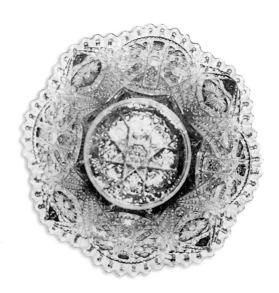

MADE BY
Imperial, 1909 – 1915

Bowl, 8" – 9"
Marigold   50

Bowl, 5½"
Marigold   20
Clambroth   30

MADE BY
Unknown, 1910 – 1920?

Tumbler, rare
Marigold   200

Wide Panel

Bowl, 7" – 10"
Marigold 40
Amethyst 100
Red 250
Marigold
  Milk Glass 125

Bowl, square, 6", scarce
Marigold 50
Clambroth 45

Bowl, master, 11" – 12"
Marigold 65
Amber 175

Bowl, console, 13"+, rare
Red 900

Plate, 6"
Marigold 25
Clambroth 25

MADE BY
Imperial, 1909 – 1915

Plate, 8"
Marigold 50
Red 200
Smoke 250

Plate, 10" – 11"
Marigold 75
White 75
Red 400
Clambroth 75

Rose bowl, 6½" – 8"
White 75

Rose bowl, giant, scarce
Marigold 150
Smoke 175

Underplate, 14" – 15"
Marigold 85
Red 750
Smoke 150

Spittoon whimsey, large, rare
Marigold 550

Spittoon whimsey, medium, rare
Marigold 400

Spittoon whimsey, small, rare
Marigold 200

MADE BY
Jenkins, 1920s

Pitcher with lid, rare

Marigold	1,200
White	195

MADE BY
Northwood, 1910 – 1914

Pitcher, tankard
Marigold	200
Amethyst	275
Green	300

MADE BY
Dugan, 1910

Vase, squat, 4" – 6"
Marigold	30
Amethyst	100
Peach Oplaescent	65

Vase, standard, 7" – 12"
Marigold	25
Amethyst	75
Blue	150
Peach Oplaescent	50
Aqua	165

Spittoon whimsey, from vase, 5½", rare
Peach Opalescent	125

Wigwam

Heisey, 1920s

Tumbler, rare
Marigold   150

MADE BY
Westmoreland, 1910 – 1912?

Powder jar with lid
Marigold   450

Powder jar variant, with lid
Blue Opalescent   425

Wild Grape

MADE BY
Unknown, 1910 – 1915?

Bowl, 8¾", very scarce
 Marigold   125

MADE BY
Phoenix, 1920s

Cider pitcher, rare
Iridized Moonstone   520

Compote, covered, rare
Iridized Moonstone   295

Creamer, rare
Iridized Moonstone   150

Goblet
Peach Opalescent   150

Sugar, rare
Iridized Moonstone   100

Wine
Marigold   145

Wild Rose Wreath

MADE BY
U. S. Glass, 1914 – 1915

Basket
    Blue Opalescent   450

Nut cup, stemmed, rare
    Marigold   575
    White   700

MADE BY
Fenton, 1915

Cider pitcher, scarce
Marigold   450

Compote, ruffled, rare
Marigold   150

Wine goblet
Marigold   90
Blue   100
Aqua Opalescent   600
Aqua   145